HELOCs for Real Estate Investors

How to Buy, Rehab, and Scale Property Using Home Equity

By Joseph G. Correa

Licensed Mortgage Broker, Finibi Mortgage

Copyright & Legal Notice

First Edition, 2026

Table of Contents

Foreword

Real estate has always been the fastest and most reliable wealth-building vehicle in history, but most people never experience its true power because they are trapped on the wrong side of financing. They save for years to come up with a down payment, struggle to qualify for traditional loans, and then wait months for approvals while the best deals disappear. Meanwhile, experienced investors quietly use a different system, one that lets them move faster, buy more property, and recycle the same money over and over again. That system is not secret, illegal, or reserved for the wealthy. It is home equity, and specifically, the strategic use of a Home Equity Line of Credit. In this book, you are about to step into the real game of real estate investing, where speed, liquidity, and leverage determine who wins, and where HELOCs become the engine that powers growth instead of a tool people fear.

If you have already read Book 1 and Book 2 in this series, you now understand how HELOCs work and how to qualify for them. That knowledge alone puts you far ahead of the average homeowner. But this book is where everything changes. This is where home equity stops being theoretical and becomes a living, breathing financial weapon. For real estate investors, a HELOC is not just a loan, it is a revolving pool of capital that can be deployed into deals, paid back, and deployed again. It is the difference between buying one property every few years and building a portfolio of cash-flowing assets that grows month after month. I have personally watched investors go from owning a single home to controlling millions of dollars in real estate simply by mastering this one tool and using it correctly.

What makes HELOCs so powerful for investors is that they break the traditional bottlenecks of real estate. Normally, you need a down payment, closing costs, and months of underwriting to buy each property. With a properly structured HELOC, you already have the capital sitting there, ready to be used the moment a deal appears. You can make cash offers, negotiate better prices, close in days instead of weeks, and outcompete buyers who are waiting on banks. You can fund renovations without hard money loans, avoid high interest private lenders, and maintain full control of your projects. This book will show you how investors use HELOCs to execute strategies like BRRR, fix-and-flip, buy-and-hold, and even creative financing in ways that banks never teach.

I want to be clear about something very important. Using home equity for investing is not about gambling or taking reckless risks. It is about using capital that is already tied up in your property and putting it to work in income-producing assets. The biggest mistake homeowners make is letting hundreds of thousands of dollars sit idle while inflation quietly erodes its value. Meanwhile, rents rise, property values climb, and opportunities pass them by. Investors do not let their equity sleep. They turn it into rental income, appreciation, tax advantages, and long-term wealth. When done correctly, this strategy does not increase financial stress, it reduces it by replacing dead equity with cash-flowing assets that pay for themselves.

Throughout my career as a licensed mortgage broker at Finibi Mortgage, I have structured HELOCs for homeowners, business owners, and investors across Florida and beyond. I have seen firsthand how the same person, with the same income and the same house, can end up either financially stuck or financially free depending on how they use their equity. The difference is not intelligence, luck, or timing. It is strategy. This book is built on real underwriting rules, real lending guidelines, and real-world investing principles that actually work in today's market. There is no hype here, no unrealistic promises, and no dangerous shortcuts. What you will find is a blueprint that shows how to move from one property to many while keeping risk controlled and cash flow growing.

One of the most misunderstood aspects of using HELOCs for investing is the idea of leverage. Leverage scares people because they have been taught that all debt is bad. In reality, there is a massive difference between consumer debt and strategic investment leverage. Credit cards and car loans drain your income. Investment leverage, when used correctly, creates income. A HELOC tied to your home, when deployed into rental property or profitable projects, becomes a bridge between where you are today and the financial future you want. The goal is not to borrow forever. The goal is to use borrowed money to acquire assets that pay off the borrowing and leave you with lasting wealth.

This book will also show you how to structure your investing so that your HELOC does not stay maxed out. One of the most powerful features of a HELOC is that it revolves. That means when you use it to buy or rehab a property and then refinance, sell, or stabilize the property, you pay the line back and regain your available credit. Now you can do it again. This is how investors scale without constantly needing new down payments. It is how one property becomes two, two become five, and five become a portfolio that produces income whether you work or not.

You will also learn how to avoid the common traps that hurt investors. Many people misuse their HELOCs by funding lifestyle purchases, leaving balances high, or failing to plan their exits. That is not investing, that is financial self-sabotage. This book will walk you through how to analyze deals, plan your capital stack, manage draws, and protect your primary residence while still using it to create wealth. Real estate investing should make your life more secure, not more stressful. When done correctly, your properties should pay your HELOC, your HELOC should fund your next deal, and your net worth should rise every year.

The beauty of this strategy is that it works whether you are just starting or already experienced. If you own a home with equity, you already have the seed capital to become an investor. You do not need private lenders, partners, or massive savings. You need education, discipline, and the right financial structure. That is exactly what this book provides. You are not just learning about loans, you are learning how to build a personal banking system using your home as the foundation.

By the time you finish this book, you will see your house differently. It will no longer be just a place to live. It will be a financial engine, a source of opportunity, and a launchpad for building a portfolio that can support your family for decades. The same tool that banks use to grow wealthy is now available to you, and this book will show you how to use it with precision, confidence, and clarity. Welcome to the world of investor-grade home equity, where your first property becomes the key that unlocks many more.

Chapter 1

The Investor's Banking System — Turning Home Equity Into Unlimited Deal Flow

Real estate investors who scale quickly do not think in terms of savings accounts, down payments, or traditional mortgages. They think in terms of liquidity, velocity, and access to capital. The moment you understand this shift, everything changes. The wealthy do not grow because they earn more; they grow because they control capital that can be deployed instantly. A HELOC allows a homeowner to turn trapped equity into a private revolving credit facility that behaves like a bank account, but one that is backed by property rather than income alone. Instead of waiting to qualify for every new purchase, the investor with a HELOC already has buying power available before a deal even appears.

The traditional real estate investor waits for approval, orders appraisals, submits tax returns, and hopes underwriting agrees with their numbers. This creates delays, missed deals, and weak negotiating power. The HELOC investor operates differently. Because the line is already approved and sitting open, it can be used to write cash offers, fund rehabs, cover down payments, or even purchase properties outright. This speed creates leverage. Sellers prefer cash buyers. Contractors move faster when they know funds are available. Refinances happen smoothly when the purchase and rehab are already completed. The HELOC does not replace mortgages; it becomes the fuel that makes them work.

When structured properly, a HELOC creates what professional investors call a "recycling engine." Money leaves the HELOC to acquire or improve property. That property is then refinanced or sold. The proceeds return to the HELOC. The available credit is restored. The same dollars are used again. This is how investors scale without needing new savings. It is not about borrowing more; it is about using the same money more efficiently. Most homeowners only use their equity once when they sell. Investors use the same equity over and over again to build wealth.

The reason this works is because real estate produces two powerful forces at the same time: cash flow and appreciation. Cash flow pays expenses and loans. Appreciation increases equity. When you combine these forces with a revolving credit line, you get compounding growth. Each deal increases your borrowing base, which increases your ability to buy more property, which increases cash flow, which pays off debt faster. This is how one house quietly becomes a portfolio. The HELOC investor is not focused on interest rates the way traditional borrowers are. They are focused on spreads. If a HELOC costs 8% and a rental produces a 14% return, the investor keeps the difference. If a flip earns $50,000 and the HELOC interest cost is $7,000, the investor keeps $43,000. The cost of capital matters, but what matters more is whether that capital creates more money than it costs. That is what makes debt productive instead of destructive.

Another critical shift is understanding that a HELOC is not a mortgage replacement. It is a bridge. It bridges you from opportunity to permanent financing. Investors use HELOCs to buy properties quickly, renovate them, increase their value, and then refinance into long-term fixed loans. The HELOC gets paid back. The property remains. The cash flow continues. This allows an investor to grow without permanently tying up their credit line. It becomes a deal conveyor belt.

Many people fear using their home as a financial tool, but banks have been doing exactly that for centuries. They borrow against assets to buy income-producing assets. When you do it responsibly, your house becomes a wealth generator instead of a passive asset. You are not risking your home by investing; you are using your home to reduce financial dependence on any single income source. This book is not about speculation. It is about structured investing. Every HELOC-funded deal must have an exit. The exit might be a refinance, a sale, or rental stabilization. The numbers must support it. When done correctly, the HELOC never stays high for long, but your property count keeps rising. That is the heart of the investor's banking system.

Practical Example: *Using a HELOC to Buy, Rehab, and Recycle Capital*

Let's walk through a simple example using realistic numbers to show exactly how this works. Imagine a homeowner owns a primary residence worth $500,000 and owes $250,000 on their mortgage. That means they have $250,000 in equity. A bank allows them to access 80% of the home's value, which is $400,000. Since the existing mortgage is $250,000, the maximum HELOC they qualify for is $150,000. This $150,000 is not a loan that starts charging interest. It is a credit line that only costs money when it is used.

An investor finds a distressed rental property selling for $120,000. The property needs $30,000 in repairs. The total project cost is $150,000. The investor uses their HELOC to fund the entire purchase and rehab. The $120,000 purchase is paid in cash from the HELOC. The $30,000 rehab is drawn over time as contractors complete the work. The HELOC balance is now $150,000. After the rehab, the property is worth $220,000 based on an appraisal. The investor applies for a new rental mortgage at 75% loan-to-value. Seventy-five percent of $220,000 is $165,000. The bank issues a new mortgage for $165,000 on the rental property. That $165,000 is paid to the investor at closing. The investor uses $150,000 of it to pay off the HELOC balance completely. The remaining $15,000 is cash profit.

Now let's look at what the investor owns. They have a rental property worth $220,000. They have a mortgage on it for $165,000. Their equity in that property is $55,000. Their HELOC is back to zero balance with the full $150,000 available again. They also have $15,000 in cash that can be used for reserves or the next deal.

Next, the rental produces $2,000 per month in rent. The new mortgage payment is $1,100. Taxes, insurance, and maintenance are $400. That leaves $500 per month in positive cash flow. That $500 can be saved, used to pay down debt, or applied to the HELOC on the next deal.

The investor has now turned $150,000 of home equity into a $220,000 asset that pays $500 per month and created $55,000 in new equity. They did not lose their HELOC. They recycled it. The same $150,000 is ready to be used again.

If this process is repeated four times, the investor could own four rental properties worth nearly $900,000 while still having access to their original HELOC. Each property produces income. Each refinance pays back the credit line. Each cycle builds wealth.

This is how investors scale without saving new money. They are not creating debt; they are converting equity into income-producing property. The math is simple, but the impact is massive. Home equity becomes the engine. Real estate becomes the fuel. Cash flow becomes the reward.

This is the professional investor's banking system, and once you understand it, you never look at your house the same way again.

Chapter 2

Deal Selection and Equity Multiplication — Choosing Properties That Turn HELOCs Into Wealth

Using a HELOC to invest in real estate does not make you rich by itself. What makes the strategy powerful is pairing cheap, flexible capital with properties that multiply equity and produce income. This chapter focuses on the most important skill any HELOC-based investor must develop: choosing the right deals. You can have a $300,000 line of credit, but if you deploy it into the wrong property, you will tie up your capital, increase risk, and slow your progress. When you deploy it into the right property, your line of credit becomes a wealth-building machine.

The first rule of HELOC investing is that every property must improve your financial position the moment it stabilizes. That means the property must either create equity, create cash flow, or ideally both. Equity comes from buying below market value and improving the property. Cash flow comes from rents exceeding all expenses, including debt. A good HELOC deal creates new equity that replaces the equity you used and cash flow that services all debt so you are never forced to feed the investment from your personal income. Professional investors do not buy based on emotion or aesthetics. They buy based on math. The most powerful metric is what the property will be worth after repairs, not what it costs today. This is known as the after-repair value. If a property is worth $250,000 after being fixed and you can buy and rehab it for $170,000, you have created $80,000 of equity. That equity becomes the foundation for your refinance, which is what allows you to pay back your HELOC and reuse it.

Cash flow is equally important. The property must generate enough rent to cover the new mortgage, taxes, insurance, maintenance, and a buffer. If the property cannot do this, it will drain your finances and reduce your ability to invest again. A HELOC investor is not trying to own property for the sake of ownership. They are building a self-funding system where every property pays for the next one.

Location matters, but not in the way most people think. Investors using HELOCs do not need luxury neighborhoods or trendy areas. They need stable rental demand, affordable prices, and properties that can be improved. Working-class neighborhoods, small multifamily properties, and older homes often offer the best opportunities because they allow value to be added through repairs and management. Another key principle is liquidity. You want properties that lenders like. That means single-family homes, duplexes, and small residential rentals. These are easy to refinance. Exotic properties, mixed-use buildings, and unusual assets may look exciting, but they are harder to finance, which makes it harder to get your HELOC money back out.

When analyzing a deal, the HELOC investor always asks three questions. How much will this be worth when it is fixed? How much will it cost me all-in? How much will it cash flow when it is rented? If those three numbers work, the deal works. If any of them are weak, the deal is rejected. This discipline is what separates investors who grow from those who get stuck.

One of the biggest advantages of using a HELOC is that it allows you to move quickly on distressed properties. Many of the best deals never hit the open market because they are bought by cash buyers. With a HELOC, you become that cash buyer. You can negotiate better prices, demand seller concessions, and close before other buyers even get approved. This increases your equity from day one.

As your portfolio grows, each successful deal increases your net worth and your borrowing power. Banks love investors who own multiple cash-flowing properties. That means your refinance options improve, your rates improve, and your leverage improves. This creates a positive feedback loop where each deal makes the next one easier.

This chapter is not about luck. It is about repeating a process that turns your HELOC into a long-term wealth engine. When you choose properties that produce equity and income, your HELOC becomes a tool for growth rather than a liability.

Practical Example: *How One Smart Deal Turns $100,000 of Equity Into $300,000 of Property*

Imagine an investor has a HELOC with a $100,000 limit. They find a small rental property listed for $130,000 that needs $20,000 in repairs. The property will be worth $200,000 once fixed based on comparable sales in the area. The total cost of the project is $150,000. The investor uses $100,000 from the HELOC and $50,000 from savings or a partner to fund the deal.

The property is purchased for $130,000. The rehab costs $20,000. The all-in cost is $150,000. After the rehab, the property is appraised at $200,000. A lender offers a refinance at 75% loan-to-value. Seventy-five percent of $200,000 is $150,000. That means the bank issues a new mortgage for $150,000.

At closing, the investor receives $150,000. They use $100,000 to pay off the HELOC completely. They use the remaining $50,000 to repay their partner or replenish their savings. The HELOC is now back to zero balance with the full $100,000 available again. The investor now owns a rental property worth $200,000 with a $150,000 mortgage. Their equity in the property is $50,000. They did not leave any of their own money stuck in the deal. The HELOC has been recycled. The property is rented for $1,800 per month. The mortgage payment is $950. Taxes, insurance, and maintenance are $450. That leaves $400 per month in positive cash flow.

That $400 per month can be used to build reserves, pay down debt, or fund the next deal. Meanwhile, the investor has added $50,000 to their net worth through equity. Their HELOC is still intact. Their borrowing power is stronger because they now own a cash-flowing rental.

If the investor repeats this three times, they could own $600,000 in rental property with very little of their own cash invested, while still having access to their HELOC. Each property pays its own way. Each refinance restores the credit line. Each cycle multiplies wealth.

This is not speculation. This is structured investing powered by home equity. When you choose the right deals, the numbers always tell the truth. Your HELOC does not disappear. It transforms into real estate, income, and long-term financial security.

Chapter 3

Deal Engineering — Turning Ordinary Properties Into Equity Machines

Real estate investing with a HELOC is not about buying property. It is about engineering deals. Most people see a house and think in terms of bedrooms, paint color, and curb appeal. Investors using home equity see something very different. They see a financial instrument that can be restructured, improved, refinanced, and multiplied. A HELOC gives you raw capital, but deal engineering determines whether that capital grows or dies. The purpose of this chapter is to teach you how to turn ordinary, overlooked properties into equity-producing machines that replenish your HELOC while building long-term wealth.

Every engineered deal starts with understanding the spread between what a property costs today and what it will be worth after you improve it. This spread is called value creation. Value is not magic. It comes from solving problems. You are not buying houses; you are buying inefficiencies. These inefficiencies might be deferred maintenance, poor marketing, a bad tenant, outdated kitchens, or a seller who needs speed. When you solve those problems, the market rewards you with higher property value. Your HELOC is the tool that allows you to solve those problems quickly.

The most important number in deal engineering is the after-repair value. This is the realistic price the property will sell or appraise for once it is fixed and stabilized. You do not guess this number. You determine it by studying comparable sales in the area. If similar renovated homes sell for $240,000, then that is your target. Once you know that number, you work backward. You subtract what a lender will loan on a refinance, usually about 75 percent. On a $240,000 property, that would be $180,000. That $180,000 is the maximum you will be able to pull out later.

Your goal is to buy and fix the property for less than that $180,000. If you can buy and rehab it for $160,000, you have a $20,000 buffer. That buffer becomes either profit, reserves, or equity. This is how you protect your HELOC. You never want to owe more than the refinance will give you back.

Cash flow is engineered at the same time. You analyze what rents will be after the property is repaired. You subtract the new mortgage payment, taxes, insurance, maintenance, and vacancy. What remains must be positive. This positive cash flow is what keeps your system running. It pays for future HELOC interest, unexpected repairs, and growth. A property that creates equity but no cash flow will slow your ability to scale. Another layer of deal engineering is controlling how much HELOC money stays tied up. The ideal deal is one where you use your HELOC temporarily and then get it back through refinancing. You do not want to leave large balances sitting on your HELOC for years. The faster you recycle your line, the more deals you can do. Think of your HELOC as a conveyor belt. The faster deals move across it, the more wealth you generate.

This is why investors love distressed properties. Distressed sellers create discounts. Discounts create equity. Equity enables refinancing. Refinancing repays the HELOC. When you buy a perfect house at full price, you cannot create this loop. You need opportunity, not perfection.

Financing strategy matters just as much as purchase price. You must choose lenders that allow cash-out refinances on rentals, use after-repair value, and have reasonable seasoning requirements. These lenders are your partners in the recycling process. Your HELOC is only as powerful as your ability to convert it back into cash through refinancing.

Deal engineering is not risky when done correctly. It is calculated. You are not betting on appreciation. You are manufacturing equity through improvements and smart buying. Appreciation becomes a bonus instead of a requirement. This is what separates professional investors from amateurs.

By mastering this process, your HELOC becomes more than a loan. It becomes a factory. You feed it distressed property, and it produces equity, cash flow, and financial independence.

Practical Example: *How One HELOC Is Recycled Into a Growing Rental Portfolio*

Imagine a homeowner has a HELOC with a $120,000 limit. They find a small rental house listed for $135,000. The property needs $25,000 in repairs to be competitive with similar homes in the neighborhood. Based on nearby sales, once fixed it will be worth $220,000. The investor structures the deal so that the total cost is $160,000. This includes the purchase price, repairs, closing costs, and holding expenses.

The investor uses $120,000 from the HELOC and $40,000 from savings to complete the purchase and renovation. After four months, the home is fully renovated and rented. An appraiser confirms a value of $220,000. A lender offers a refinance at 75 percent loan-to-value. Seventy-five percent of $220,000 is $165,000. This means the new loan will be $165,000.

At closing, the investor receives $165,000. The first $120,000 is used to pay off the HELOC completely. The remaining $45,000 goes back to the investor's savings. The HELOC is now fully available again with a $120,000 limit. The investor now owns a rental property worth $220,000 with a $165,000 mortgage. Their equity is $55,000. The property rents for $1,900 per month. The mortgage payment is $1,050. Taxes and insurance are $300. Maintenance and reserves are $250. That leaves $300 per month in positive cash flow.

That $300 per month is now extra income. The investor's HELOC is still intact. Their net worth has increased by $55,000. Their income has increased by $3,600 per year. They can now use the same HELOC to do another deal.

If this process is repeated three times, the investor will own nearly $660,000 in real estate while still having access to the same HELOC. Each property is self-sustaining. Each refinance restores the credit line. Each deal increases wealth without requiring new savings.

This is how home equity becomes a compounding engine. You are not borrowing against your home to consume. You are borrowing against it to create assets that replace and multiply your equity. When done correctly, the math always works in your favor.

Chapter 4

The Refinance Loop — How Investors Turn HELOCs Into Permanent Wealth

The true power of using a HELOC for real estate investing is not found in buying properties. It is found in how you exit those purchases. Many people believe the deal is over once the property is acquired, but professional investors know the real profit is created when the HELOC is paid back and the property becomes self-sustaining. This process is called the refinance loop. It is the financial engine that allows you to grow without draining your own savings or permanently maxing out your home equity.

When you use a HELOC to buy or renovate a property, you are only temporarily borrowing against your home. The goal is never to leave that debt there. The goal is to move that debt onto the property itself through a refinance. In doing so, you shift the financial responsibility from your primary residence to an income-producing asset. This is the moment when risk decreases and stability increases. Your home is no longer carrying the burden of the investment. The rental property is now responsible for paying its own mortgage. The refinance loop works because lenders value stabilized rental properties differently than distressed ones. When a property is purchased in poor condition, it is not eligible for traditional financing. Once it is repaired, rented, and appraised, it becomes a bank-friendly asset. That is when long-term lenders step in. They are willing to lend based on the new, higher value and the rental income. This allows you to replace your HELOC debt with a 30-year fixed or adjustable mortgage that is designed for long-term holding.

One of the biggest mistakes new investors make is refinancing too early or too late. Refinancing too early means the property has not reached full value or stable rent, which limits how much cash you can pull out. Refinancing too late means your HELOC stays maxed out longer than necessary, increasing interest costs and limiting your ability to invest again. The correct timing is when the property is fully renovated, fully rented, and ready to be appraised at its highest supported value.

Understanding loan-to-value ratios is critical. Most lenders will refinance rental properties at around 70 to 75 percent of the appraised value. That means if your property is worth $200,000, the maximum loan will be between $140,000 and $150,000. Your job as an investor is to structure the deal so that this loan is enough to pay back the HELOC. If it is not, you have trapped capital, which slows your growth. This is why buying below market value and adding value through renovations is so important. Appreciation alone is slow and uncertain. Manufactured equity is immediate and controllable. When you buy a property for $130,000 that will be worth $200,000 after $20,000 of repairs, you have created $50,000 of equity. That equity is what makes the refinance work.

Cash flow also improves after the refinance. HELOCs usually have variable rates and interest-only payments. Rental mortgages have lower rates and longer terms. When you refinance, your monthly payment typically drops, which increases cash flow. This is another way the refinance loop strengthens your financial position.

The refinance loop also improves your credit profile. Each successful refinance adds a new mortgage that is paid on time by rental income. This builds a strong track record with lenders. Over time, this allows you to access better loan terms, higher limits, and more flexible financing. Your financial reputation grows alongside your portfolio.

As you repeat this loop, your HELOC becomes a revolving door rather than a dead end. Money goes out to buy and fix properties. Refinances bring the money back. Properties remain. Income increases. Equity compounds. This is how investors scale without hitting a wall.

The refinance loop is not about gambling on rising prices. It is about controlling your exits. When you plan every deal around how the HELOC will be paid back, you protect your home, your credit, and your future.

Practical Example: *How One HELOC Creates a Self-Funding Real Estate Portfolio*

Imagine an investor has a HELOC with a $150,000 limit. They find a neglected rental property listed for $140,000. The property needs $30,000 in repairs. Comparable renovated homes in the area sell for $240,000. The investor uses the HELOC to fund the entire project, drawing $140,000 to purchase the home and $30,000 over time for renovations. The total HELOC balance is $170,000, but the HELOC limit is only $150,000, so the investor covers $20,000 from savings.

After four months, the property is fully renovated and rented for $2,000 per month. An appraisal confirms a value of $240,000. The investor applies for a rental refinance. The lender offers 75 percent loan-to-value. Seventy-five percent of $240,000 is $180,000. This becomes the new loan amount.

At closing, the lender issues $180,000. The investor uses $150,000 to pay off the HELOC completely. They use $20,000 to reimburse their savings. The remaining $10,000 is profit. The HELOC is now back to zero balance with the full $150,000 available again. The investor now owns a rental property worth $240,000 with a mortgage of $180,000. Their equity in the property is $60,000. The new mortgage payment is $1,150 per month. Taxes and insurance are $350. Maintenance and reserves are $300. Total expenses are $1,800. Rent is $2,000, leaving $200 per month in positive cash flow.

The investor has created $60,000 in equity, $10,000 in cash, and $2,400 per year in income without leaving their HELOC tied up. They can now use the same $150,000 to do another deal.

If this process is repeated four times, the investor could own nearly $1 million in real estate with the same HELOC. Each property stands on its own. Each refinance repays the line. Each deal increases wealth.

This is how home equity becomes permanent financial leverage. Not by borrowing once, but by recycling capital again and again until the portfolio funds itself.

Chapter 5

Risk Control and Capital Protection – Using Home Equity Without Gambling Your Future

Using a HELOC for real estate investing creates powerful leverage, but leverage must always be paired with control. The difference between a professional investor and someone who loses money is not access to capital, it is how that capital is protected. This chapter is about making sure your HELOC builds wealth without putting your primary residence, credit, or financial stability at risk. When risk is managed correctly, leverage becomes safe. When risk is ignored, leverage becomes dangerous.

The first rule of HELOC risk management is that your primary home is not the investment. Your investment properties are. That means your HELOC must always be treated as temporary capital. It should never be left maxed out for long periods of time, and it should never be used for properties that cannot repay it. Every deal must be structured with a defined exit that moves the debt from your home to the property itself through refinancing or sale. This is how you separate your personal life from your investing activity. Another major risk is over-leveraging. Just because a bank gives you access to

$200,000 of equity does not mean you should use all of it at once. Professional investors keep reserves. They leave room on their HELOC in case of repairs, vacancies, or market shifts. Using 60 to 70 percent of your available credit is much safer than using 100 percent. This buffer is what prevents small problems from becoming financial emergencies.

Cash flow is your second layer of protection. A property that does not produce positive cash flow is a liability. Even if it creates equity, it will strain your finances. Cash flow covers repairs, interest, and unexpected events. When every property in your portfolio pays you every month, stress disappears. When properties require you to feed them, risk increases.

Interest rate risk is also important. HELOCs usually have variable rates. This means payments can increase when rates rise. This is why you never want to leave large balances on your HELOC for long. The refinance loop protects you by moving debt to long-term fixed loans. The HELOC is just the bridge.

Diversification is another form of risk control. You do not want all of your equity tied up in one property or one market. Smaller properties spread risk. If one tenant leaves, you still have others. If one house needs repairs, your other rentals keep producing income. Liquidity is also part of safety. You should always have access to cash or unused credit. This gives you flexibility. It allows you to handle emergencies without selling assets or missing payments. Your HELOC is part of your liquidity system, but only if it is not maxed out.

Finally, you must respect numbers. Hope is not a strategy. Every deal must be based on conservative assumptions. Rents should be realistic. Repairs should include buffers. Appraisals should be supported by solid comparables. When numbers are honest, risk is predictable. When numbers are optimistic, risk becomes invisible until it is too late.

This chapter is not about fear. It is about control. When you understand how to protect your capital, your HELOC becomes a tool for freedom rather than a source of stress.

Practical Example: *How Risk Management Keeps an Investor Safe Even When Things Go Wrong*

Imagine an investor has a $200,000 HELOC. Instead of using the full amount, they decide to limit themselves to $140,000, leaving $60,000 unused as a safety buffer. They purchase a rental property for $110,000 and spend $25,000 on repairs, for a total cost of $135,000. They use the HELOC to fund the project, leaving $5,000 of available credit still unused.

After repairs, the property is worth $190,000. A lender offers a refinance at 75 percent loan-to-value. Seventy-five percent of

$190,000 is $142,500. That is enough to pay off the $135,000 HELOC balance and leave $7,500 in cash. The HELOC is restored to zero with the full $200,000 limit available again.

The rental produces $1,700 per month. The new mortgage payment is $900. Taxes and insurance are $300. Maintenance and reserves are $250. Total expenses are $1,450. Cash flow is $250 per month.

Now imagine the tenant leaves and the property sits vacant for two months. That is $3,400 in lost rent. Repairs cost another $2,000. The total hit is $5,400. Because the investor left $60,000 unused on their HELOC and has cash flow from other properties, this problem is easily handled without stress.

If the investor had used the full $200,000 HELOC on one deal, they would have no buffer. A vacancy could force missed payments. But because they respected leverage limits, the system remains stable.

This is how professionals survive market shifts. They do not avoid risk. They control it. When you protect your HELOC, your portfolio can grow safely for decades.

Chapter 6

Scaling With Precision — How to Grow From One Property to a Portfolio Using a Single HELOC

The most misunderstood part of HELOC investing is scale. Many homeowners believe a HELOC allows them to buy one investment property. In reality, a properly managed HELOC can support the purchase of many properties over time. The key is not the size of the HELOC. The key is how efficiently it is recycled. Scaling is not about borrowing more money; it is about moving the same money faster and safer through profitable deals. This chapter explains how professional investors use one line of credit to build a growing portfolio without constantly increasing risk.

The foundation of scaling is velocity. Velocity means how quickly your HELOC moves from available credit to property and back to available credit again. The faster this loop occurs, the more times you can deploy your capital. An investor who recycles a $100,000 HELOC once per year can buy one property per year. An investor who recycles that same HELOC three times per year can buy three properties with the same capital. Speed creates scale. Refinancing is what resets the system. Every time you refinance a completed project, the

HELOC is restored. This gives you the same buying power you had before, but now you also own an income-producing asset. That asset increases your net worth, improves your credit profile, and strengthens your ability to borrow in the future. Over time, your borrowing base grows, which allows you to take on larger or multiple projects simultaneously.

Cash flow is what makes scaling sustainable. A portfolio that grows without cash flow becomes fragile. A portfolio that produces surplus income becomes stronger every month. Cash flow pays HELOC interest, funds repairs, and builds reserves. It also allows you to withstand vacancies or market slowdowns without panic.

Scaling also requires discipline. Not every deal should be done. As your portfolio grows, the cost of mistakes increases. This means you must be even more selective with properties, conservative with numbers, and careful with leverage. Professional investors grow slowly at first and then accelerate as their systems become stronger.

Another key to scaling is diversification. You do not want all your properties in one street, one tenant base, or one price range. Mixing single-family homes, duplexes, and small rentals spreads risk and creates stability. Your HELOC becomes the common funding source, but your income comes from many places.

Eventually, your portfolio begins to feed itself. The combined cash flow from multiple rentals can begin paying down mortgages, funding new purchases, or even paying off your HELOC faster. This is when you move from investor to operator. You are no longer dependent on your job or your home. Your properties become your financial engine.

Scaling with a HELOC is not reckless when done correctly. It is controlled expansion. Each property adds strength. Each refinance restores liquidity. Each month of cash flow increases stability. This is how ordinary homeowners quietly build extraordinary wealth.

Practical Example: *How One $100,000 HELOC Becomes a $1 Million Portfolio*

Imagine an investor has a $100,000 HELOC. They find a distressed rental property for $95,000 that needs $20,000 in repairs. The total project cost is $115,000. The property will be worth $170,000 once renovated. The investor uses the HELOC and $15,000 in savings to complete the deal.

After repairs, the home is appraised at $170,000. A lender offers 75 percent loan-to-value, which is $127,500. The investor uses $100,000 to pay off the HELOC and $15,000 to repay their savings. The remaining $12,500 is profit. The

HELOC is now restored to full capacity.

The property rents for $1,600. The mortgage is $850. Taxes, insurance, and maintenance are $450. Cash flow is $300 per month.

The investor repeats this process four times. Each time, the HELOC is recycled and a new property is added. After four deals, the investor owns $680,000 in property, has over $100,000 in equity, and earns about $1,200 per month in cash flow.

As rents increase and mortgages are paid down, the portfolio becomes stronger. The investor can now qualify for additional lines of credit, commercial loans, or larger projects. What started as one HELOC has become a long-term wealth machine.

This is how scale is created. Not by luck. Not by speculation. But by disciplined recycling of home equity into income-producing assets that grow stronger every year.

Chapter 7

The Exit Strategy Blueprint — How to Lock In Profits and Protect Your Equity for Life

Real estate investors who succeed for decades all have one thing in common: they plan their exits before they ever buy a property. When you are using a HELOC, exit strategy is not optional. It is the foundation of safety, profit, and long-term control. A HELOC is a temporary tool. The property is permanent. This chapter explains how to design exits that lock in wealth, stabilize cash flow, and prevent your home from ever being at risk.

The most common exit strategy in HELOC investing is the refinance. You buy a property using your HELOC, improve it, raise its value, rent it, and then replace the HELOC with a long-term mortgage. This moves the debt from your personal home to the investment property. That one action dramatically reduces risk because your home is no longer tied to the deal. The rental now pays for itself. Your HELOC is restored. Your net worth increases.

Another exit strategy is selling. Some properties are best used for short-term profit. You buy them below market value, fix them, and sell them. The profit pays off the HELOC and leaves cash behind. That cash can be used as reserves or combined with your HELOC for larger deals. This is called capital stacking. It allows you to grow your buying power faster than relying on equity alone.

The best investors combine both strategies. Some deals are kept as rentals. Others are flipped. The goal is to always keep your capital moving while your asset base grows. You do not get rich by holding everything or selling everything. You get rich by choosing the right exit for each deal.

Timing matters. You want to refinance when the property is fully stabilized and valued at its peak. You want to sell when the market supports your profit. You do not want to hold HELOC balances while waiting for hope. The exit should be mechanical, not emotional.

Debt structure is also part of the exit. When you refinance, you should aim for fixed-rate or predictable loans. HELOCs float with interest rates. Long-term mortgages give you stability. This turns volatile leverage into predictable payments that can be covered by rent.

Your exit strategy also affects taxes. Rental refinances are usually not taxable because you are borrowing, not selling. Sales may create capital gains. A smart investor uses refinances to access capital tax-free and sells selectively when needed. This keeps more money working instead of being paid to taxes.

The final goal is not just profit. It is permanence. Your HELOC gives you speed. Your exits give you security. When these work together, your home becomes the launchpad for a portfolio that can last generations.

Practical Example: *How a Smart Exit Turns One HELOC Into Long-Term Financial Security*

An investor has a $150,000 HELOC. They find a distressed duplex selling for $140,000. The duplex needs $40,000 in repairs. After renovation, it will be worth $280,000. The total project cost is $180,000. The investor uses $150,000 from the HELOC and $30,000 from savings.

After six months, the duplex is fully renovated and rented. Each unit rents for $1,500, producing $3,000 per month. The property appraises at $280,000. A lender offers a refinance at 75 percent loan-to-value. Seventy-five percent of $280,000 is $210,000.

At closing, the investor receives $210,000. The HELOC balance of $150,000 is paid off. The $30,000 from savings is reimbursed. That leaves $30,000 in profit. The investor now owns a duplex with a $210,000 mortgage. The new mortgage payment is $1,350. Taxes and insurance are $400. Maintenance and reserves are $450. Total expenses are $2,200. Rent is $3,000. Cash flow is $800 per month.

The investor now has $800 per month in income, $70,000 in equity, and their full $150,000 HELOC restored. Their home is no longer carrying the debt. The investment pays for itself.

This is the power of exit planning. The HELOC was the tool. The refinance was the lock. The cash flow is the reward.

Chapter 8

From Investor to Empire Builder — Using HELOC-Powered Real Estate to Create Permanent Wealth

At a certain point in every successful investor's journey, something important changes. They stop thinking about individual deals and start thinking about systems. The HELOC is not just a way to buy property; it is the foundation of a private banking system that allows you to grow, protect, and control wealth for decades. This chapter explains how investors transition from owning a few properties to building a long-term real estate empire powered by home equity and disciplined capital management.

When you own one or two rentals, success is measured by cash flow and appreciation. When you own many, success is measured by stability, liquidity, and scalability. This means your portfolio must be designed to survive downturns, vacancies, interest rate changes, and personal life events without collapsing. Your HELOC plays a critical role in this because it remains your emergency liquidity source even as your properties grow. A professional portfolio is layered. You do not just own houses. You own cash-flowing assets, equity-rich assets, and liquid credit. The HELOC sits at the center of this structure. It allows you to respond to opportunities quickly, handle emergencies without selling property, and continue growing even when the market changes. Investors who fail usually fail because they run out of liquidity, not because their properties are bad.

As your portfolio expands, your HELOC strategy also evolves. You may add additional HELOCs on other properties. You may convert equity into business lines of credit. You may begin using portfolio loans or commercial financing. But it all starts with the discipline you learned using your first HELOC. That discipline becomes the DNA of your empire.

Another key shift is that your income becomes diversified. Instead of relying on one job or one tenant, you now have income coming from multiple properties. This reduces financial stress and increases long-term security. It also allows you to reinvest more aggressively because your lifestyle is no longer dependent on any single source of money.

Tax strategy becomes more powerful as well. Rental income, depreciation, refinances, and capital gains rules all work in your favor when used correctly. A HELOC allows you to access capital without selling assets, which often means you can grow without triggering taxes. This keeps more money compounding inside your portfolio. Legacy is the final piece. A properly structured HELOC-powered portfolio is not just for you. It can support your family, fund education, and create generational wealth. Real estate is one of the few assets that can be passed down while still producing income. When you build with discipline and planning, you are not just investing. You are building a financial institution that your family controls.

This is what separates someone who owns rentals from someone who owns a real estate empire. The HELOC is the doorway. The system is what carries you through.

Practical Example: *How One HELOC Becomes a Multi-Property Wealth Engine*

An investor begins with a $120,000 HELOC on their primary home. Over three years, they complete three successful refinance cycles. Each cycle results in a new rental property that produces $350 per month in net cash flow and holds $50,000 in equity.

After three cycles, the investor owns three rental properties. Each one is worth $220,000. The total portfolio value is $660,000. Each property has a mortgage of $170,000. Total debt is $510,000. Total equity is $150,000. Monthly cash flow is $1,050.

The investor also still has their $120,000 HELOC available

because each refinance paid it back. This gives them liquidity and growth capital at the same time.

Now imagine a recession causes rents to drop by 10 percent. Each rental now produces $315 per month instead of $350. Total cash flow becomes $945. The portfolio is still profitable. Mortgage payments are still covered. The HELOC is untouched.

If a major repair of $15,000 is needed on one property, the investor can use the HELOC to cover it and then pay it back from cash flow over time. They do not have to sell anything or panic.

This is what empire-level investing looks like. The HELOC is no longer just a loan. It is the backbone of a self-sustaining financial system that keeps growing, even when conditions change.

Chapter 9

Cash Flow Engineering – Turning Equity Into Monthly Income Without Selling Your Assets

At the highest level of real estate investing, the true goal is not owning property. The goal is controlling income. Property is simply the machine that produces that income, and a HELOC is the ignition key that starts the engine. This chapter explains how experienced investors design portfolios that transform trapped home equity into stable, growing monthly cash flow without ever giving up ownership of their assets.

Most people think wealth comes from appreciation. In reality, appreciation is unpredictable. Cash flow is what gives you freedom. Cash flow pays your bills, funds new investments, and protects you when the market shifts. A HELOC allows you to accelerate the creation of cash-flowing assets instead of waiting years to save enough money for each purchase. By front-loading your investing with equity, you move into income much faster.

Cash flow engineering begins with selecting properties that support strong rent-to-price ratios. You are not looking for the prettiest houses. You are looking for properties where the rent covers all expenses and still leaves a surplus. This surplus is what makes the HELOC strategy sustainable. If your properties do not pay more than they cost, your equity will slowly bleed away.

When you use a HELOC, you temporarily increase your expenses because HELOC interest begins immediately. This is why speed matters. The faster you complete the renovation and refinance, the faster you replace high-interest HELOC debt with low-interest rental mortgages. Once this happens, your monthly expenses drop and your cash flow rises.

Another powerful concept is cash-on-equity return. This measures how much income your properties produce relative to the equity you used. If you use $100,000 of equity to create $12,000 per year in income, that is a 12 percent return. That is far higher than most traditional investments. This is why home equity, when deployed correctly, is one of the most powerful wealth tools available.

As your portfolio grows, your cash flow compounds. One property may produce $300 per month. Five properties may produce $1,500. Ten may produce $3,000. Over time, that income can replace a job, fund retirement, or pay off your home. This is what financial independence looks like.

A HELOC allows you to reach this point years faster than saving alone. It is not risky when paired with cash-flowing assets. It is simply using existing wealth to create new income.

Practical Example: *How $120,000 of Equity Becomes $3,000 Per Month in Income*

An investor has a $120,000 HELOC. They use it to complete three BRRR-style deals over two years. Each deal requires about $120,000 temporarily but is refinanced and paid back.

Each property ends up worth $200,000 and carries a $150,000 mortgage. Each rents for $1,900 per month. The mortgage payment is $950. Taxes and insurance are $300. Maintenance and reserves are $250. That leaves $400 per month per property.

After three deals, the investor owns three rentals producing $1,200 per month. Their HELOC is still intact at $120,000. Their total portfolio value is $600,000. Their total debt is $450,000. Their equity is $150,000.

The investor repeats this three more times. Now they own six rentals producing $2,400 per month. Their HELOC remains available. Their equity grows with each refinance.

This is how trapped equity becomes permanent income. The HELOC started the process. Cash flow now sustains it.

Chapter 10

Leverage Without Fear — How to Use Debt as a Tool Instead of a Trap

Debt is the most misunderstood tool in personal finance. Most people are taught that debt is dangerous and should be avoided. In reality, what is dangerous is unproductive debt. Productive debt, when used correctly, is one of the greatest accelerators of wealth ever created. HELOC-powered real estate investing sits at the center of this principle. This chapter explains how professional investors use leverage safely, predictably, and profitably without putting their homes or futures at risk.

The difference between destructive debt and productive debt is simple. Destructive debt buys things that go down in value and do not produce income. Productive debt buys assets that create cash flow and equity. A HELOC used for consumption weakens you. A HELOC used for rental property strengthens you. The money is the same. The outcome is completely different.

Professional investors never ask, "How much can I borrow?" They ask, "How much can this asset safely support?" A rental property that produces $2,000 per month in rent can only support so much debt. If the mortgage, taxes, insurance, and maintenance cost $1,600, there is $400 of margin. That margin is safety. That margin protects against vacancies, repairs, and interest rate changes. If there is no margin, there is risk.

HELOCs amplify leverage, which is why discipline is essential. The line gives you immediate access to capital, but that capital must be deployed into deals that increase net worth and cash flow. Every draw on a HELOC should be tied to an asset that will eventually replace that debt with long-term financing or profit. If you cannot see how the HELOC will be paid back by the property, you should not do the deal.

Another important concept is leverage stacking. This happens when you have multiple layers of debt on the same asset. A HELOC on your home plus a mortgage on a rental plus a credit card for repairs creates fragile leverage. Professional investors simplify. They use the HELOC temporarily and then remove it through refinancing. Long-term debt stays with the rental. Short-term debt disappears.

Interest rate management is also part of safe leverage. HELOC rates change. Rental mortgages are more stable. The refinance loop protects you from rate spikes. The faster you move debt from your HELOC to fixed or predictable loans, the safer your system becomes.

Psychology also matters. Investors who fear debt hesitate and miss opportunities. Investors who respect debt move with confidence. The goal is not to avoid leverage. The goal is to control it. When leverage is attached to income-producing property, it becomes an ally instead of an enemy.

Over time, leverage actually decreases. As rents rise and mortgages are paid down, your loan-to-value drops. Your equity increases. Your risk declines. What began as a leveraged investment becomes a powerful, debt-free asset in the long run.

This is how investors use debt to get rich while others use debt to stay poor. The HELOC is not the danger. Misuse is.

Practical Example: *How Safe Leverage Builds Wealth Instead of Stress*

An investor has a $180,000 HELOC on their home. Instead of using all of it, they limit themselves to $120,000 for any single deal. They buy a distressed rental for $100,000 and spend $20,000 on repairs. The property is now worth $180,000.

They refinance at 75 percent loan-to-value. Seventy-five percent of $180,000 is $135,000. That loan pays off the

$120,000 HELOC balance and leaves $15,000 in cash. The HELOC is restored to $180,000.

The property rents for $1,700. The new mortgage is $950. Taxes and insurance are $300. Maintenance and reserves are $250. Total expenses are $1,500. Cash flow is $200 per month.

The investor now owns an $180,000 asset with $45,000 in equity and positive cash flow. Their HELOC is still fully available. Their risk is low because the property pays for itself.

This is leverage done correctly. Debt created income. Equity increased. Liquidity remained. That is how professionals win.

Chapter 11

The Infinite Equity Loop — How to Turn One Home Into a Lifetime of Real Estate Wealth

Everything you have learned in this book comes down to one powerful idea: your home is not just where you live, it is the financial engine that can build your entire investment future. The Infinite Equity Loop is the process of turning a single property into a permanent source of capital, income, and control. This chapter ties together HELOCs, deal selection, refinancing, cash flow, and risk management into one repeatable wealth system.

Most people use home equity once in their lifetime when they sell their house. Investors use it over and over again while they continue to own the house. This is possible because equity is not destroyed when you borrow against it if that borrowing creates more equity somewhere else. When a HELOC funds a rental that is refinanced, the equity moves from one property to another. You are not consuming wealth, you are relocating it into assets that produce income.

The Infinite Equity Loop works because each deal strengthens the system. Every refinance restores your HELOC. Every new rental adds income. Every payment reduces debt. Over time, the portfolio becomes safer even though it started with leverage. This is the opposite of consumer debt, which becomes more dangerous over time.

The loop also creates optionality. You can stop at any time. You can sell properties. You can pay off your home. You can live off cash flow. The power of the system is not that you must keep borrowing forever. It is that you always have the choice.

Most financial systems are fragile. They depend on a job, a market, or a single asset. A HELOC-powered real estate portfolio is antifragile. When rents rise, you benefit. When values rise, you benefit. When inflation hits, debt becomes easier to pay. You own assets that adapt to the economy.

This is why banks, corporations, and institutions use this same model. They borrow against assets to buy more assets. The difference is that now, homeowners can do it too.

When you understand the Infinite Equity Loop, you stop chasing money and start building systems that produce it. That is true financial freedom.

Practical Example: *How One Home Creates a Self-Funding Real Estate Empire*

An investor owns a home worth $500,000 with a $250,000

mortgage. They open a HELOC for $150,000. Over five years, they complete five BRRR-style deals. Each deal creates a rental worth $220,000 with a $165,000 mortgage and $55,000 in equity. Each produces $350 per month in cash flow.

After five deals, the investor owns $1.1 million in rental property. Total mortgages are $825,000. Total equity is $275,000. Monthly cash flow is $1,750.

The investor still has their $150,000 HELOC available because each deal paid it back through refinancing. Their primary home has appreciated to $600,000. Their total net worth is now over $600,000 higher than when they started.

This is not luck. This is the Infinite Equity Loop. One house became many. One line of credit became a lifetime income stream. This is the power of using home equity the smart way.

Chapter 12

The Investor's Financial Command Center — How to Monitor, Optimize, and Protect Your HELOC-Powered Portfolio

Once an investor owns multiple properties funded through HELOC cycles, the game changes. You are no longer simply acquiring assets; you are managing a financial ecosystem. Cash is moving between properties, mortgages, credit lines, rents, repairs, and reserves. Without a system to monitor this flow, even profitable portfolios can become fragile. This chapter explains how professional investors build a financial command center that allows them to see everything clearly, make better decisions, and protect what they have built.

The first principle of a command center is visibility. You must know exactly how much is owed on every mortgage, how much is available on every HELOC, how much cash is in reserves, and how much income is coming in every month. Wealth is not created by numbers in isolation; it is created by how those numbers interact. A portfolio that looks strong on paper can collapse if liquidity is weak. A portfolio with modest equity but strong cash flow and reserves can survive almost anything. The HELOC is the nervous system of this financial body. It connects all parts of your portfolio. When a property needs a repair, the HELOC can fund it. When a new deal appears, the HELOC can seize it. When rents come in, they can flow back to reduce balances or increase reserves. But if you do not track balances and usage carefully, the HELOC can become overloaded. That is why professional investors set rules for how much of their HELOC can be used at any one time and how quickly it must be replenished.

Cash flow is the heartbeat of the system. Every month, rents should exceed expenses. That surplus should be divided intentionally. Some of it goes to reserves. Some goes to paying down debt. Some may go to funding new opportunities. Without a plan, surplus cash disappears. With a plan, surplus becomes growth.

Another key part of the command center is stress testing. This means asking what would happen if rents dropped, interest rates rose, or vacancies increased. You run the numbers in advance. If your portfolio survives these scenarios on paper, it will survive them in reality. This is how investors avoid panic and forced sales.

Technology makes this easier than ever. Simple spreadsheets, budgeting software, and online banking allow you to see your entire empire on one screen. When you know where everything is, you are in control. When you guess, you are gambling.

The final layer of the command center is planning. You are not just tracking the past. You are projecting the future. How much equity will you have in five years? How much cash flow? How much debt will be paid down? These projections guide your decisions today.

This is how investors move from chaos to mastery. They stop hoping their portfolio works and start knowing it does.

Practical Example: *How a Simple Financial Command Center Prevents Disaster and Increases Wealth*

An investor owns four rental properties. Each is worth $200,000. Each has a mortgage of $150,000. Total property value is $800,000. Total debt is $600,000. Total equity is $200,000. The investor also has a $120,000 HELOC that is currently unused.

Each property rents for $1,800. Total rent is $7,200 per month. Mortgage payments are $1,000 per property, totaling $4,000. Taxes and insurance are $300 per property, totaling $1,200. Maintenance and reserves are $200 per property, totaling $800. Total expenses are $6,000. Cash flow is $1,200 per month.

The investor sets a rule that at least $600 per month goes into reserves. After one year, reserves grow to $7,200. The remaining $600 per month is used to pay down mortgages or fund opportunities.

Now imagine two tenants leave and one property needs a $10,000 roof. That is $3,600 in lost rent plus $10,000 in repairs, totaling $13,600. Because the investor has reserves and a HELOC, they handle the situation without missing payments or selling assets.

The portfolio remains intact. Cash flow recovers. Equity continues to grow. The command center did its job.

This is how professional investors stay wealthy. They do not rely on luck. They rely on systems.

Chapter 13

Legacy Wealth & Exit Mastery – Turning HELOC-Powered Real Estate Into Generational Income

At the highest level of investing, the goal is no longer simply to own property or generate cash flow. The real objective is permanence. You want a system that produces income, protects capital, and can be passed on to your family without disruption. When HELOC-powered real estate is structured correctly, it becomes one of the most powerful legacy vehicles ever created. This chapter explains how to convert a growing rental portfolio into a long-term family wealth engine that works for decades without depending on your labor.

Legacy investing begins with separating ownership from operation. The properties may be managed by you today, but they must be able to operate without you tomorrow. That means stable tenants, professional property management, predictable financing, and documented systems. When your rentals are self-sustaining, your heirs are not inheriting a job, they are inheriting a financial machine.

Debt management is a critical part of legacy planning. HELOCs are temporary tools. Rental mortgages are long-term structures. Over time, rents rise while mortgage payments stay the same. This naturally increases cash flow and reduces risk. Eventually, many properties become free and clear. At that point, income becomes nearly pure profit. This is when generational wealth becomes unstoppable.

Another pillar of legacy is liquidity. A portfolio that only produces rent but has no access to capital is fragile. HELOCs on your primary home and eventually on rental properties give your family access to cash without selling assets. This allows them to pay taxes, handle repairs, and invest in new opportunities while keeping ownership intact.

Tax efficiency also compounds wealth. Refinancing is not taxable income. Depreciation shelters rental profits. Estates can pass property to heirs with stepped-up basis. When these rules are combined, real estate becomes one of the most tax-advantaged assets in the world.

The final step is documentation. Your strategy, accounts, contacts, and processes must be written down. When this is done, your family does not inherit confusion. They inherit clarity.

This is how HELOC investing evolves into legacy wealth. Not through speculation, but through structure.

Practical Example: *How One HELOC Becomes a Multi-Generational Income System*

An investor builds a portfolio of six rental properties using HELOC recycling. Each property is worth $220,000. Total portfolio value is $1,320,000. Each property has a mortgage of $160,000. Total debt is $960,000. Total equity is $360,000.

Each property rents for $1,900 per month. Total rent is $11,400. Total mortgage payments are $6,000. Taxes, insurance, and maintenance are $3,000. Cash flow is $2,400 per month or $28,800 per year.

After 15 years, rents increase while mortgages are paid down. Two properties are fully paid off. Cash flow rises to $4,000 per month.

The investor also maintains a $150,000 HELOC for liquidity.

Their children inherit properties that generate income, have low debt, and include a built-in credit system for emergencies and growth.

This is what real legacy looks like. One home became a permanent financial foundation for generations.

Chapter 14

The Investor's Flywheel — How HELOC-Powered Real Estate Compounds Faster Every Year

At a certain stage of investing, something powerful begins to happen. Growth stops being linear and becomes exponential. This is called the flywheel effect. A flywheel is a heavy wheel that takes effort to start, but once it is spinning, it gains momentum and requires less energy to keep moving. HELOC-powered real estate works the same way. Early deals require planning, discipline, and patience. Later, the system begins to feed itself. Cash flow increases, equity expands, and opportunities become easier to capture. This chapter explains how to intentionally design and accelerate that flywheel.

The flywheel starts with three forces working together: equity, income, and access to credit. Equity gives you borrowing power. Income gives you stability. Credit gives you speed. When all three grow together, your financial engine becomes unstoppable. A HELOC ties all three together because it allows you to convert equity into income and then use that income to increase equity and access even more credit. The most important concept in the flywheel is reinvestment. Every dollar of cash flow that is not consumed can be used to strengthen the system. It can be added to reserves, used to pay down mortgages, or combined with your HELOC to fund new deals. Over time, small surpluses become large capital pools. That is when growth accelerates.

As your portfolio grows, your borrowing power also increases. Banks look at your rental income, your property values, and your payment history. They are more willing to extend additional credit, offer better rates, and approve larger loans. This creates a virtuous cycle. Strong performance leads to more capital. More capital leads to more deals. More deals lead to stronger performance.

Another flywheel effect comes from inflation. As rents rise and mortgage payments stay fixed, cash flow increases. As property values rise, equity increases. Both of these strengthen your HELOC position. Inflation, which hurts savers, rewards asset owners.

The investor who understands the flywheel does not rush. They build momentum. They focus on quality deals, stable cash flow, and disciplined use of leverage. When the flywheel is spinning, wealth compounds faster than most people imagine.

This is how small beginnings turn into financial independence. Not through luck, but through momentum.

Practical Example: *How the Flywheel Turns $100,000 of Equity Into Millions Over Time*

An investor starts with a $100,000 HELOC. They complete two deals per year. Each deal produces a rental worth $200,000 with $50,000 in equity and $300 per month in cash flow.

After one year, they own two rentals. Total equity is $100,000. Cash flow is $600 per month.

After three years, they own six rentals. Total equity is $300,000. Cash flow is $1,800 per month.

Their increased equity allows them to increase their HELOC to $200,000. Now they can do larger deals or multiple deals at once.

By year five, they own ten rentals. Total equity is $500,000. Cash flow is $3,000 per month.

The flywheel is now spinning. They are no longer limited by savings. Their own system funds growth.

This is how HELOC investing evolves from a single strategy into a self-sustaining wealth engine.

Chapter 15

Financial Independence on Autopilot – Living Off HELOC-Built Cash Flow Without Selling Assets

The final evolution of HELOC-powered real estate is not endless growth. It is control. When your portfolio produces more income than you need to live, you have achieved financial independence. At that point, you no longer need to trade time for money, sell properties, or take financial risks just to survive. Your HELOC-built portfolio becomes a personal pension that you control. This chapter explains how to transition from growth mode into income mode without breaking the system that created your wealth.

Many investors make a fatal mistake when they reach this stage. They stop thinking strategically and begin consuming their portfolio. They sell properties to fund lifestyle or reduce debt too aggressively, weakening the income engine. A smarter approach is to let the assets do what they were designed to do: produce cash flow. The goal is not to liquidate wealth. The goal is to live off the yield while the principal continues to grow.

Your HELOC remains a powerful tool even in this stage. It becomes a liquidity buffer instead of a growth engine. Instead of funding new acquisitions, it provides emergency capital, tax payments, renovation funds, and opportunity capital. This means you can live comfortably without selling property when unexpected expenses arise.

Portfolio optimization also becomes important. Not all properties perform equally. Some produce more cash flow. Some hold more equity. Over time, you may sell underperformers and reinvest into stronger assets. This keeps your income growing while your workload decreases.

Debt continues to work in your favor. As inflation raises rents and mortgage balances shrink, your cash flow increases automatically. Your real debt burden decreases every year. This is why long-term fixed mortgages are so powerful. They lock in yesterday's cheap dollars while today's rents keep rising.

Tax efficiency becomes another pillar of independence. Depreciation shields rental income. Refinances provide tax-free access to capital. Strategic sales are used only when beneficial. This allows you to keep more of what you earn.

True financial independence is not about never working. It is about never being forced to work. A HELOC-built real estate portfolio gives you that freedom.

Practical Example: *How a HELOC Portfolio Replaces a $150,000 Salary*

An investor has built a portfolio of eight rental properties over ten years. Each property is worth $240,000. Total portfolio value is $1,920,000. Each property has a mortgage of $140,000. Total debt is $1,120,000. Total equity is $800,000.

Each property rents for $2,100 per month. Total rent is $16,800. Mortgage payments total $7,200. Taxes, insurance, and maintenance total $4,000. Net cash flow is $5,600 per month or $67,200 per year.

Rents increase 3 percent per year. After five years, rent rises to about $2,435 per property. Total rent becomes $19,480. Expenses rise slowly. Net cash flow becomes about $7,200 per month or $86,400 per year.

The investor also keeps a $150,000 HELOC as a liquidity buffer.

This income replaces most jobs, continues to rise, and never requires selling the properties. This is what living off your equity truly means.

Chapter 16

The Forever Wealth Strategy — How HELOC Real Estate Turns Into a Self-Sustaining Financial Empire

At the highest level of financial mastery, wealth is no longer about accumulation. It is about sustainability. The Forever Wealth Strategy is the system that allows everything you have built with HELOC-powered real estate to continue producing income, opportunity, and security for the rest of your life and beyond. This chapter explains how investors move from active building into permanent control, where money, not effort, does the work.

The foundation of forever wealth is structural strength. Your portfolio must be able to withstand recessions, vacancies, interest rate cycles, health events, and changes in your personal life without forcing you to sell assets. That strength comes from three things: low effective leverage, high cash flow, and access to liquidity. The HELOC gives you liquidity. The rentals give you cash flow. Time gives you lower leverage as debt is paid down and values rise.

As years pass, inflation quietly works in your favor. Your mortgage payments stay fixed while rents increase. What once felt like heavy leverage becomes light. A $1,200 mortgage that felt tight early on becomes insignificant when rent rises to $2,500. This creates margin. Margin creates freedom.

The smartest investors also restructure over time. They refinance strategically, consolidate loans, and sometimes pay off high-interest debt early. The goal is not to be debt-free as fast as possible. The goal is to be cash-flow rich while maintaining flexibility. Debt that is cheap and tied to productive assets is not a burden. It is a tool.

Your HELOC evolves at this stage. It is no longer used to buy property. It becomes your family bank. It provides liquidity for opportunities, emergencies, tax payments, or strategic investments without disturbing your income-producing assets. You no longer think of it as debt. You think of it as stored financial power.

The final layer of forever wealth is governance. You document everything. Properties are held in proper entities. Trusts, wills, and succession plans are in place. Your family knows how the system works. This ensures your empire continues even if you are not there to run it.

This is what it means to truly own wealth. You do not worry about money. Money works for you.

Practical Example: *How One HELOC Creates a Permanent Family Financial System*

An investor has spent 20 years building a HELOC-powered portfolio. They own 10 rental properties. Each is worth $300,000. Total value is $3,000,000. The mortgages have been paid down to $1,200,000. Total equity is $1,800,000.

Each property rents for $2,500 per month. Total rent is $25,000. Mortgage payments are $8,000. Taxes, insurance, and maintenance are $6,000. Net cash flow is $11,000 per month or $132,000 per year.

The investor also maintains a $250,000 HELOC on their primary residence and one rental. This is their liquidity reserve.

They live comfortably on $80,000 per year and reinvest the rest. Their properties continue to appreciate. Their debt continues to shrink.

Their children inherit properties that produce income, have low leverage, and include built-in access to capital through HELOCs.

This is not retirement. This is financial immortality built from one home.

Final Thoughts

The most important realization you can walk away with from this book is that your financial future is not determined by how much money you earn, but by how well you control capital. For most people, their largest untapped source of capital is sitting quietly inside their home, locked behind a mortgage they make every month but rarely question. This book was written to help you unlock that capital, not recklessly, but with strategy, discipline, and purpose. A HELOC is not a gamble. It is a financial lever. When you pull that lever in the right direction, it multiplies opportunity, speed, and wealth.

Real estate has always been the great equalizer. It allows ordinary people to participate in extraordinary financial growth using leverage that is not available in most other investments. But leverage without knowledge leads to loss. This is why this series exists. You now understand how HELOCs work, how to qualify for them, how to deploy them into real estate, how to recycle them through refinancing, and how to manage risk while doing so. You have learned not just what to do, but how and why it works. That is what turns information into power.

What separates successful investors from everyone else is not intelligence or timing. It is execution with patience. HELOC investing rewards those who follow the system, run the numbers honestly, and allow compounding to do its work. You do not need to do dozens of deals per year. You only need to do a few good ones consistently. Over time, equity grows, cash flow rises, and debt becomes lighter. Eventually, the system begins to feel effortless. That is when financial stress disappears.

One of the most liberating aspects of HELOC-based investing is that it removes dependence on external permission. You do not need to beg banks for every deal. You do not need partners to get started. You do not need massive savings. You already have the seed capital. You simply needed the knowledge to use it properly. That is what this book gives you.

As your portfolio grows, you will also notice something else changing. Your mindset will shift. You will stop seeing your home as an expense and start seeing it as a financial asset. You will stop fearing debt and start respecting leverage. You will stop thinking about paychecks and start thinking about cash flow. These shifts are subtle, but they are powerful. They are what separate people who struggle financially from people who quietly build wealth over time.

This book was not written to impress. It was written to equip. You now have a blueprint that can be applied in almost any market, in almost any economy. Homes may rise and fall in value, interest rates may move, and rents may fluctuate, but the system of buying below value, adding value, refinancing, and recycling capital remains timeless. This is how banks, corporations, and wealthy families have built fortunes for generations. Now you have access to the same playbook.

The greatest danger is not that you will fail. The greatest danger is that you will do nothing. Knowledge without action is wasted potential. Even a small HELOC, used correctly, can change your life over the next decade. One deal becomes two. Two become five. Five become a portfolio that supports you and your family for years to come.

Your house is not just where you live. It is the doorway to a different financial future. Walk through it with confidence.

How to Get a Personalized HELOC Review

If you found *HELOC Fundamentals: How Home Equity Lines of Credit Really Work — and How to Use Them Safely* helpful, you may want to see how these concepts apply to your own home, credit profile, and financial goals.

Every homeowner's situation is unique. Home value, mortgage balance, credit history, income type, and state-specific lending rules all affect how much equity you can access, what type of HELOC you may qualify for, and what terms may be available. The examples in this book are designed to teach how HELOCs work — but your real options can only be determined by reviewing your actual numbers.

If you would like a **no-obligation Home Equity Line of Credit review**, you can request one here:

Website:https://www.nodocsheloc.com

Email:info@FinibiMortgage.com

A licensed mortgage broker will review your information and explain what HELOC and home equity options may be available to you based on your specific situation.

No cost. No pressure. No obligation.

Joseph G. Correa

About the Author

Joseph G. Correa is a licensed mortgage broker and the founder of Finibi Mortgage, a Florida-based brokerage specializing in home equity, real estate investment financing, and alternative lending strategies for homeowners, business owners, and investors. With more than two decades of experience in mortgage lending, underwriting, and financial structuring, Joseph has helped thousands of borrowers access capital using intelligent, low-risk leverage rather than high-interest consumer debt.

Unlike traditional loan officers who focus only on closing transactions, Joseph's approach is rooted in long-term financial strategy. He believes that mortgages, HELOCs, and credit lines should be used as tools for building wealth, protecting cash flow, and creating financial resilience — not as traps that keep families locked into decades of unnecessary interest payments. This philosophy has made him a trusted advisor for entrepreneurs, real estate investors, and self-employed borrowers who need flexible, modern financing solutions that banks often fail to provide.

Joseph is widely known for his expertise in home equity lines of credit, no-documentation and bank-statement loan programs, investor financing, and creative equity-based strategies such as debt-elimination systems and capital recycling. His ability to translate complex lending rules into simple, actionable guidance has helped homeowners turn idle equity into productive capital for investments, businesses, and passive income.

Through his education platform, Finibi Academy, Joseph has trained tens of thousands of students worldwide in credit, mortgage strategy, real estate financing, and financial independence. His courses and books are used by first-time homeowners, seasoned investors, and financial professionals seeking a clearer, more honest understanding of how modern lending really works.

Joseph created *The Home Equity Wealth Series* to give everyday homeowners the same financial knowledge that banks, hedge funds, and institutional investors use to control capital and minimize risk. His mission is simple: to help people stop guessing, stop fearing debt, and start using smart leverage to build real financial freedom.

When he is not structuring loans or writing, Joseph works with families and investors across the United States to design personalized equity strategies that align with their goals, cash flow, and long-term wealth plans.

The Home Equity Wealth Series Roadmap

The Professional Guide to Using Your Home to Build Financial Freedom

The purpose of *The Home Equity Wealth Series* is to give homeowners the same financial tools and strategies used by banks, investors, and institutions–translated into clear, practical guidance for everyday people. Each book builds on the last, taking you from basic understanding to advanced mastery of how to use home equity safely, intelligently, and profitably across every stage of life.

Book 1 — *HELOC Fundamentals*This book gives you the foundation. You will understand how Home Equity Lines of Credit work, how they are structured, how risk is controlled, and how equity becomes usable capital. The books that follow are designed to help you apply that knowledge to your own situation, your income type, your credit profile, and your long-term financial goals.

Book 2 — *How to Qualify for a HELOC* This book shows you how lenders actually evaluate borrowers. You will learn how credit scores, income, property type, and debt ratios affect approval, limits, and interest rates. You will also learn how to position yourself to qualify for the largest possible credit line at the best possible terms.

Book 3 — *HELOCs for Real Estate Investors* This book focuses on using home equity to buy, rehab, refinance, and scale rental properties. It explains how investors use HELOCs for down payments, renovations, and portfolio growth while keeping cash flow positive and risk controlled.

Book 4 — *Self-Employed HELOC Strategies* Designed for business owners, freelancers, 1099 borrowers, and LLCs, this book explains how bank-statement income, business income, and alternative documentation can be used to qualify for home equity even when traditional tax returns do not reflect true cash flow.

Book 5 — *Credit Mastery for HELOC Approval* This book dives deep into credit strategy. You will learn how utilization, credit mix, and reporting behavior affect HELOC limits and pricing—and how to optimize your credit profile specifically for home equity approval.

Book 6 — *No-Doc & Alternative HELOC Programs* This book covers asset-based HELOCs, no-income-verification options, and non-traditional lending programs for high-net-worth, self-employed, or cash-heavy borrowers who do not fit inside standard underwriting models.

Book 7 — *Using a HELOC to Eliminate Debt* This book teaches how to use home equity to replace high-interest credit cards, personal loans, and auto loans with low-interest revolving credit, allowing borrowers to eliminate debt years faster and save tens of thousands of dollars in interest.

Book 8 — *Using a HELOC to Build Wealth* This book shows how homeowners fund investments, businesses, and passive income streams using HELOCs while maintaining liquidity and controlling risk.

Book 9 — *HELOC Risk Management* This book focuses entirely on safety. You will learn how to structure buffers, cash-flow coverage, rate protection, and leverage limits so your home becomes safer over time—not more vulnerable.

Book 10 — *The Smart Borrower's Home Equity Blueprint* The final book ties everything together into a complete lifetime strategy for using home equity as a personal banking system, investment engine, and financial safety net.

Book 11 — *The Cashflow Accelerator Method*

The Cashflow Accelerator Method is the final transformation stage of *The Home Equity Wealth Series*. While the earlier books teach how to access, qualify for, and safely use home equity, this book teaches how to **weaponize cash flow itself** to permanently eliminate debt and create lasting wealth. Together, these books are designed to turn a single asset—your home—into a lifelong financial advantage. Each volume adds another layer of understanding, allowing you to move from homeowner to capital manager, from borrower to strategist, and from financial stress to long-term stability.

This is not about taking more risk.It is about learning how money really works—and using that knowledge to build financial freedom that lasts.

Educational & Financial Disclaimer

This book is provided for **educational and informational purposes only**. The author and publisher are not engaged in rendering legal, tax, accounting, investment, or financial advice. Although the author is a licensed mortgage broker, the information in this book is intended to provide general education about Home Equity Lines of Credit (HELOCs) and home equity strategy, not personalized financial, legal, or lending advice.

Mortgage programs, underwriting guidelines, interest rates, credit requirements, and home equity products vary by lender, investor, state, and economic conditions, and may change at any time without notice. The examples, calculations, and scenarios presented in this book are hypothetical and are for illustration only. They do not represent guaranteed outcomes or actual loan approvals.

Before making any financial decisions, including applying for a HELOC, refinancing, borrowing against home equity, or using credit for investment or debt repayment, readers should consult with a qualified mortgage professional, financial advisor, tax advisor, or attorney who can evaluate their specific situation.

Risk Disclosure

Borrowing against home equity involves risk. A HELOC is secured by your home, which means failure to make required payments could result in foreclosure or loss of property. This book teaches responsible, conservative, and structured use of home equity, but no financial strategy is risk-free.

Readers are solely responsible for their financial decisions. Neither the author nor the publisher makes any warranties, express or implied, about the accuracy, completeness, or applicability of the information in this book to any individual or situation.

www.ingramcontent.com/pod-product-compliance
Ingram Content Group UK Ltd.
Pitfield, Milton Keynes, MK11 3LW, UK
UKHW020157290926
15471UKWH00005B/920

9 798295 573934